BLUE
AND
WHITE
DONE
RIGHT

BLUE
AND
WHITE
DONE
RIGHT

*The Classic Color
Combination for
Every Decorating Style*

BY HUDSON MOORE
WRITTEN BY MARIO LÓPEZ-CORDERO

SCHUMACHER

IT'S A MATCH MADE IN HEAVEN, A CLASSIC PAIRING, THE DESIGN WORLD EQUIVALENT OF MILK AND COOKIES—OR BETTER YET, CHAMPAGNE AND CAVIAR. THE ORIGINS OF WHAT MOST OF US CONSIDER THE BLUE-AND-WHITE ARCHETYPE—CHINESE PORCELAIN—CAN ACTUALLY BE TRACED BACK TO ANCIENT MESOPOTAMIA, WHERE CRAFTSPEOPLE FIRST DEVISED BLUE POTTERY GLAZES TO IMITATE THE LOOK OF LAPIS LAZULI, THAT SEMIPRECIOUS MINERAL PRIZED BY *HOMO SAPIENS* SINCE NEOLITHIC TIMES. BUT IT WASN'T UNTIL THE NINTH CENTURY THAT ARTISANS IN THE ABBASID CALIPHATE (CENTERED IN MODERN-DAY IRAQ), THEMSELVES IMITATING WHITE POTTERY IMPORTED FROM CHINA (IT WAS ACTUALLY MORE GRAY THAN PURE WHITE), ADDED FLOURISHES TO THEIR WARES WITH LOCALLY SOURCED COBALT, INNOVATING ON THE SEDUCTIVE COLOR COMBINATION. IT'S THAT SAME ABBASID COBALT—PLUS A LITTLE DARK AGES CROSS-POLLINATION—WE HAVE TO THANK FOR THE CLASSIC LOOK OF YUAN AND MING PORCELAIN, THE NE PLUS ULTRA OF THE BLUE-AND-WHITE GENRE.

TO MAKE A LONG STORY SHORT, ABBASID COBALT FOUND ITS WAY TO CHINA VIA THE SILK ROAD, WHERE IT SERENDIPITOUSLY MET WITH THE INVENTION OF PORCELAIN IN JINGDEZHEN A FEW CENTURIES LATER. THE NEWLY WROUGHT JINGDEZHEN CERAMIC WAS VITREOUS, SONOROUS, AND—UNLIKE THE EARTHENWARE POTTERY IN USE UP TO THAT POINT—TRULY,

The yen for blue and white goes back centuries. Case in point: The Porcelain Room at Drottningholm Palace in Sweden, designed to display King Oscar II's vast collection of faience and completed in 1897.

At Charlottenhof Palace in Potsdam, Germany, built in
the mid-19th century, a ticking stripe cheerfully covers every
surface of the "Siam's Tent" room—a space that continues
to influence countless contemporary decorators. OPPOSITE:
In the hands of the Swedes, blue and white reached
stupendous heights, shown here in another grand residence,
Tureholm Castle (dating back to 1745), where patterns
in Chinese export porcelain inspired trompe l'oeil murals.

PRISTINELY WHITE. IT SO HAPPENS THAT COBALT IS ONE OF THE FEW PIGMENTS THAT CAN STAND THE HIGH FIRING TEMPERATURES REQUIRED OF PORCELAIN WITHOUT THE NEED OF A SECOND FIRING. WHEN THAT DEEP, RICH COBALT MET THAT CRISP, BRIGHT WHITE, A STAR WAS BORN. THE REST, AS THEY SAY, IS HISTORY.

AS YOU'LL SEE IN THESE PAGES, BLUE AND WHITE CAN BEND TO AN IMPROBABLY WIDE RANGE OF STYLES, CONFIGURATIONS, AND SCHEMES, FROM TRADITIONAL TO CONTEMPORARY, SWEET TO SOPHISTICATED, AND EVERYTHING IN BETWEEN. TRUTH BE TOLD, THE COMBINATION'S CALM-INDUCING SENSE OF ORDER PROBABLY GOES BACK EVEN FURTHER THAN ANCIENT MESOPOTAMIA. JUST LOOK UP ON A LATE-SUMMER DAY WHEN COTTON-BALL CLOUDS PUFF ACROSS THE WIDE SWATH OF A CERULEAN SKY. OR IMAGINE THE DUSKY, IMPOSSIBLY RICH NAVY BLUE OF THE MEDITERRANEAN SWEEPING ACROSS TIDE-WASHED LIMESTONE IN AN AEOLIAN COVE. THE ALLURE OF BLUE AND WHITE IS, QUITE SIMPLY, ELEMENTAL, AND LIKE MANY THINGS BORN OF THE EARTH, EXACTS ON US A SUBLIME, INSTINCTUAL PULL. IN OTHER WORDS, ASKING WHY BLUE AND WHITE IS SO SEDUCTIVE IS LARGELY IRRELEVANT: ALL WE REALLY NEED TO DO IN THE FACE OF SUCH BEAUTY IS JUST DIVE IN AND SURRENDER.

Blue and white wasn't just a fad for northern climes: azulejos, or hand-painted tiles, emblazon an 18th-century Carmelite convent in Porto, Portugal, showcasing the captivating quality that Chinese export porcelain had throughout the world.

POWDER

A dusty, diffuse shade originally derived from the use of powdered smalt (crushed cobalt glass) as a bluing agent to brighten whites when laundering.

SKY

The scattering of sunlight through the atmosphere favors tones with the shortest wavelengths, making this the hue of the heavens.

CORNFLOWER

Johannes Vermeer was so enamored of the hue—made from costly lapis lazuli— he went into debt to create masterpieces like *Girl With a Pearl Earring*.

SLATE

Silt from seas flecked with carbon—the detritus of ancient life—gives this stone its blue-gray hue.

DELFT

In the 17th century, Dutch artisans sought to mimic the depth of Chinese porcelain by covering their tin-glazed pottery with a heavy clear coat.

SAPPHIRE

The prized gem can be found in a range of colors, but the standard reflects a velvety twilight blue.

NAVY

The shipshape shade of British Royal Navy uniforms chosen by George II in 1748 after a habit worn by the duchess of Bedford caught his fancy.

PRUSSIAN

The moody, inky shade of Picasso's Blue Period (and the standard "blue" in blueprints) was invented by accident at the dawn of the 18th century in Berlin.

PEACOCK

Is it any wonder that a crowd of peafowl is called an ostentation? The showy tone has been used as the process-blue ink in four-color printing.

A LITTLE **GLOSSARY** OF BLUES

FRENCH
A midtoned shade that emblazons the coat of arms of French kings, French national soccer jerseys, and French racing cars.

DENIM
The washed-and-worn, gently faded look of indigo-dyed cotton, originally known as serge *de Nîmes*, whence it gets its name.

CADET
The dusky, dapper tone has been the color of choice for West Point officers-in-training since 1816.

COBALT
The OG tone of Chinese ceramics also lends its crystalline vivacity to the stained glass in Chartres Cathedral.

ULTRAMARINE
Once made from ground lapis lazuli, it lends dimension to the robes of countless Renaissance Madonnas.

INDIGO
The hue of true selvedge denim, wrought from a flowering shrub once worth its weight in gold.

TURQUOISE
Found in Egyptian tombs dating to 4000 BC, the mineral has been prized by cultures from Mesopotamia to Mesoamerica for most of human history.

ROBIN'S EGG
The hue of a songbird's eggshell, it can be found splashed on porch ceilings in the South to ward off evil spirits—originally a Gullah tradition.

CERULEAN
This particularly peaceful shade—popular with artists for painting skies—was chosen for the map-and-olive-branch logo of the United Nations.

SNOW
The frozen flakes are actually translucent, refracting light in so many directions that they diffuse the entire color spectrum to give off a pure sheen.

SMOKE
Water and carbon suspended in air create its diaphanous gray plumes, said to have magical properties in certain cleansing rituals.

PORCELAIN
Its "invention" in China was actually a centuries-long process that culminated when ground volcanic rock was mixed with kaolin clay and fired at 2650°F.

CHALK
The buff white of Dover's cliffs is composed of the calcite skeletons of countless ancient plankton.

OYSTER
A mollusk defends its tender tissue by continuously producing layers of nacre, entombing invaders in iridescence.

BEIGE
The name for this shade comes from the French, which originally referred to the color of undyed sheep's wool.

NAVAJO WHITE
The ground color of the Navajo Nation flag is a warm, pastel shade that became popular as an interior paint.

EGGSHELL
The color of a hen's ear area announces the color of her eggs—the supermarket standard being a soft off-white.

CREAM
Carotenoid pigments in grazing grass give this milky hue its distinct yellow tone.

A LITTLE **GLOSSARY** OF WHITES

ISABELLINE
Named for a 17th-century archduchess who reputedly refused to change her undergarments until the end of the siege of Ostend—which lasted three years.

ALABASTER
A translucent gypsum or calcite that glows when backlit, it was used for canopic jars in ancient Egypt and windows in Byzantine churches.

LEAD
The toxic colorant, dating back to 2300 BC, was used in cosmetics in ancient Greece, Elizabethan England, Shogun Japan—and even into the 19th century.

GREEK
The distinct whitewashed look of countless *choras* was actually dictated by the government in the 1930s due to lime plaster's antiseptic properties.

ECRU
From the French *écru*—the word for unbleached or raw—the grayish yellow approximates the dusty tone of untreated linen.

PARCHMENT
Flat, lime-bleached animal skin began to supplant rolled scrolls—which could only be made with Egyptian papyrus—in the second century BC.

IVORY
Consisting mainly of dentine, this material derived from animal tusks and teeth is now outlawed in much of the world.

MILK
Combined with lime, the dairy substance makes up the earliest man-made paint and has been found in 22,000-year-old cave art.

BONE
Calcium phosphate and collagen are responsible for the warm, off-white look of one of life's basic building blocks.

CASUAL &
CLASSIC

NOTHING SAYS EASY AND BREEZY LIKE AIRY BLUE-AND-WHITE. WORKING
IN HARMONY, THE PAIRING CAN PULL A ROOM TOGETHER IN TWO SECONDS
FLAT, UNIFYING ALL KINDS OF PATTERNS—RICH MOTIFS, ROMANTIC TOILES,
EXOTIC IKATS—WITH A RANGE OF MATERIALS: WICKER, SEAGRASS, IRON,
PLASTER, ANTIQUE BROWN FURNITURE. BLUE-AND-WHITE STRIPES, IN
PARTICULAR, PROVIDE A SENSE OF ORDER WITHOUT EVEN A WHIFF OF
STUFFINESS; THEY CAN BRING AN OTHERWISE FORMAL SETUP DOWN TO EARTH
WITH AN INSOUCIANCE THAT FEELS PERFECTLY TOSSED OFF. IT'S THE KIND
OF KICK-BACK, BAREFOOT SPLENDOR THAT NEVER GOES OUT OF STYLE.

The entry hall for a Bahamian house by Miles Redd of Redd Kaihoi has a laissez-faire but sophisticated attitude with classic Chinese urns paired with a kicky zigzag rug (*Variable by Patterson Flynn*) and a to-die-for lantern covered in perfectly imperfect, hand-painted chevron stripes. OPPOSITE: *Schumacher's Zanzibar Trellis wallpaper* and wicker give emerald damask and porcelain garniture a dose of garden-fresh air in an arrangement by Mark D. Sikes. PRECEDING PAGES: The walls and ceilings of the library-slash-guest room in Sikes's Los Angeles home are upholstered in his *Ojai Stripe fabric for Schumacher*, complete with mitered corners for a tented effect, while Pierre Frey's wavy Toile de Nantes on a slipper chair adds pizzazz to a sea of straight lines.

A swirl of patterns—including *Schumacher's Abstract Leaf wallpaper*—easily fall in line in a Palm Beach bedroom by Caroline Rafferty. A range of tonalities in the same color family sets off a grasscloth-covered headboard bracketed by wicker sconces. OPPOSITE: Heather Chadduck uses a rug with a washed and faded stripe to ground casually pulled-back curtains made from Schumacher's shapely *Katsugi print* in a Florida living room.

Rhiannon Hageman quietly—and winningly—embellishes an otherwise pared-down powder room with a dusty colorway of *Schumacher's Endimione wallpaper by Charlap Hyman & Herrero*. OPPOSITE: Walls and ceilings in a breezy ticking stripe cocoon a Houston guest room by Bruce Budd in unfussy comfort that won't soon (or ever!) go out of style.

A simple runner in *Nomad fabric by Schumacher* and diamond-patterned napkins are the only embellishments needed for a table set with succulents, sunshine, and loads of understated charm by Richard Hallberg in Montecito. OPPOSITE: In Palm Beach, Phoebe Howard tempers the frills of a romantic Indian print from Katie Leede & Company with a crisp striped rug.

Victoria Hagan augments aerial views of this Bridgehampton, New York living room with a graphic rug that features stripes in alternating widths to frame the furniture arrangement.

In Lyford Cay in the Bahamas, Miles Redd of Redd
Kaihoi stitched rugs together to create a hallway
runner that tames plaster palm fronds, powder-blue
paint, and a Louis XVI–style armchair. OPPOSITE:
Redd used a custom stripe wallpaper to a similar
effect in the foyer of a Southampton house.

Lush *Samarkand Ikat II by Schumacher* is the center of attention in the Beverly Hills living room designed by Kirsten Kelli, while a tone-on-tone stripe rounds out the setup, adroitly providing cohesion while avoiding matchy-matchy clichés.

Courtney Parker designed an entire guest room around Martyn Lawrence
Bullard's evocative large-scale *Sinhala Sidewall wallpaper for Schumacher*,
drawing on its hues for the other furnishings in the room, but keeping them
sharply tailored to achieve balance. OPPOSITE: On Cape Cod, Acquire
Design uses a similar approach with *Schumacher's Marine Toile*, referencing
the locale's history and providing an appealing sense of place.

Tom Scheerer wraps a home office and studio in Hobe Sound, Florida, entirely in *Schumacher's Katsugi*, for a grand pattern-on-pattern gesture that works thanks to a range of materials monopolizing the same hues and a few dashes of natural texture.

The decorative notes in Serena Crawford's Cape Town kitchen are played almost entirely by blue-and-white porcelain, including a mosaic backsplash composed entirely of 17th-, 18th-, and 19th-century shards she discovered on 15 years' worth of walks through the historic Groot Constantia vineyards. OPPOSITE: In a French vacation house that Jean-Louis Deniot designed for his nieces and nephews, graphic cabinet fronts and floors inspired by comic books deliciously elevate juvenile inspiration with a strict palette.

MODERN

EVEN THE BEST MODERN INTERIORS CAN SOMETIMES FEEL AUSTERE. NOT
SO WHEN BLUE AND WHITE BECOME PART OF THE EQUATION: THE DUO
LENDS A GIMMICK-FREE LIVELINESS TO ANY GENRE—AND BENDS ESPECIALLY
WELL TO A CONTEMPORARY, NO-FRILLS APPROACH. CONSIDER IT A SHORTCUT
TO KEEPING THINGS LIGHT, NO MATTER HOW STRICT THE SENSIBILITY.

A Prussian blue sofa with cushions in *Schumacher's Seashells* indoor-outdoor fabric
lends a casual nonchalance to sharp angles and contemporary art in an upstate
New York lake house. OPPOSITE: A mod squad of Saarinen tulip chairs gets the
congeniality treatment with mismatched cushions in Schumacher patterns (clockwise
from top left: *Persian Lancers*, *Serendipity*, *Maxwell*, and *Exotic Butterfly*, which
was also used for the place mats) that play along nicely, thanks to a common palette.
PRECEDING PAGES: On France's Île de Ré, a cool, constrained living room by
Jean-Louis Deniot is also blissfully comfortable with a shaggy rug and inviting seating.

A fluttering wall of *Schumacher's Exotic Butterfly* gives
this powder room in Bridgehampton, New York,
by Virginia Tupker just the right amount of oomph.
OPPOSITE: With exposed cedar lining the walls and
ceilings, Tom Scheerer is mining a minimalist Zen
aesthetic for this Sag Harbor, New York, bedroom;
the medallion patterned fabric on the headboard
and platform prevent it from feeling monastic.

A bathroom by designer Beth Barter and architect Chris Hosford composed of strong planes and muscular geometry gets a lilting uplift with *Schumacher's Blommen wallpaper*. OPPOSITE: Jean-Louis Deniot turns a classic bath with a crisp, white-painted floor and wainscoting into a memorable moment with a coat of ultramarine paint on the walls and graphic rhombille tiling in the shower niche.

GLAMOROUS

SOME SPACES CAN'T WAIT TO HOST A PARTY: THEY'RE FIZZY, FABULOUS, AND
FULL OF POSSIBILITY. INTERIORS WITH THAT KIND OF CHARISMA CAN COMPEL
WITH ANY NUMBER OF TRICKS: FANCIFUL PATTERNS, GLITTERING LACQUER,
ACRES OF FABRIC AND FRILLS, GRACEFULLY PUDDLING CURTAINS. BUT WHEN
A BEWITCHING ROOM CASTS ITS SPELL WITH BLUE AND WHITE, SOMETHING
SPECIAL HAPPENS. IT'S LIKE A MIDNIGHT BLUE TUXEDO AT THE OSCARS (SEE: RYAN
GOSLING, CHRIS EVANS, DANIEL CRAIG)—THE LOOK SUDDENLY GAINS A WHOLE
NEW LEVEL OF ELEGANCE THAT NO OTHER COLOR COMBINATION CAN QUITE
MATCH. CONSIDER IT A SORCERER'S SPELL FOR ACHIEVING SOPHISTICATION.

For the vestibule of a bedroom he designed for the Kips Bay Decorator Show House, Mark D. Sikes covered walls and ceilings in his *Ojai Stripe for Schumacher* to create a tented effect that sets the tone the minute you walk into the room. OPPOSITE: In another Kips Bay room, Sikes took the spotlight by cladding living room walls in a richly colored custom Iksel Decorative Arts wallpaper, toned down ever so slightly with powder-blue upholstery (*Schumacher's Barnett linen-cotton*). PRECEDING PAGES: On Lyford Cay in the Bahamas, Miles Redd of Redd Kaihoi worked with Amanda Lindroth to design an extravaganza of an entry hall, complete with an octagonal ceiling clad in alternating panels of blue and white fabric.

Redd reprised the tented effect for the dining room of the same
house on Lyford Cay, but went in a decidedly mod direction
with a graphic chevron fabric and seat cushions in juicy patent
leather. OPPOSITE: In another tented room by Redd, he takes
a more traditional approach, applying a classic stripe vertically
on the walls and mitering them on the ceiling. The diagonally
striped lampshades and dramatic Frances Elkins chairs add zing.

The major decorative statements in this Beverly Hills living room by Miles Redd and David Kaihoi are the contemporary art (including a Damien Hirst) and the kind of black lacquer walls you can lose yourself in; but the pops of turquoise on the lamps, sofa, and in *Redd's Cubist fabric for Schumacher* (on the slipper chairs) gives it a jolt of one-of-a-kind personality

With those black-and-white painted checkered floors, Redd's own backyard New York City terrace is undeniably dapper, but the addition of sky blue and cerulean gives it that extra secret sauce known as flair. Tablecloth in *Peacock Print*, side chairs in *Brighton Pavilion*, daybed in *Cubist*, all by *Miles Redd for Schumacher*.

Although this Salt Lake City guest bedroom has been dubbed "Nana's room" by Hillary Taylor's clients, there's nothing ostensibly "granny" about it—its pitch-perfect and daring blend of paisley (*Schumacher's Askandra Flower wallpaper*), taffeta stripes, and a blue-on-blue lamp feels youthful and fresh. OPPOSITE: Paloma Contreras's beguiling dining room for the Lake Forest Infant Welfare Designer Showhouse practically sparkles with peacock-blue upholstery (including *Cubist by Miles Redd* on the armchairs) and a wallpaper (*Eastern Eden by Iksel Decorative Arts through Schumacher*) that pulls you right in.

If a piece of formal wear could be magically morphed into an interior, it would undoubtedly look as stylish—and as sexy—as Todd Alexander Romano's New York City pied-à-terre living room.

Believe it or not, this dining room was designed by John Fowler and Bunny Mellon for her New York residence in 1966. More than 50 years later, the crosshatched walls and seemingly offhand striped curtains draped just so (note how casually they set off that Renoir) feel as fresh as ever, a testament to the philanthropist's legendary taste.

A custom-colored Ralph Lauren
tattersall covers practically every inch of
the Manhattan bedroom Virginia Tupker
designed for Derek Blasberg and Nick
Brown; the graphic pattern counters the
typical trad fabric-walls-and-canopy-bed
setup with a sharply masculine edge
that's cozy, comforting, and so very chic.

BOHEMIAN

THE WORD WAS ORIGINALLY LOBBED AS AN INSULT, USED TO DESCRIBE
SOMEONE ROOTLESS, UNTETHERED, A RULE-BREAKER MOVING OUTSIDE
THE BOUNDS OF CONVENTION. BUT IS IT ANY WONDER THAT BOHEMIANISM
QUICKLY BECAME SYNONYMOUS WITH ROMANTICISM? DRAWING ON WHAT
WAS ONCE CONSIDERED EXOTIC, THE AESTHETIC BORROWS FROM EVERY
CULTURE, PULLS EQUALLY FROM THE NATURAL WORLD, AND BLENDS IT ALL
TOGETHER WITH A HIPPIE-CHIC HEEDLESSNESS THAT CARES NOT A WHIT FOR
THE WAY THINGS ARE "SUPPOSED" TO BE DONE. DISTILL IT DOWN TO A BLUE-
AND-WHITE PALETTE, AND ALL THAT PATTERN-ON-PATTERN PIZZAZZ LOOKS
POSITIVELY FATED. WHO KNEW BREAKING THE RULES COULD BE SO BEAUTIFUL?

You might not think that small-scale florals, punchy geometrics, and abstract botanicals could be successfully swirled together, but that's just what Jacqueline Coumans did using blues and whites in her Southampton, New York, guest bedroom. OPPOSITE: Fellow rule-breakers Kirsten Kelli use the same approach to make ikat, plaid, and Delft tulipieres get along exceedingly well in the Dallas home of Gerald and Kelli Ford. PRECEDING PAGES: A painted dado gives structure to a profusion of hand-painted and hand-blocked botanical motifs at Bar Palladio in the Narain Niwas Palace Hotel in Jaipur, designed by Marie-Anne Oudejans.

The pièce de résistance in a Southampton bedroom by Stewart Manger is a scenic wallpaper with an elaborate Mughal motif that Manger frames with white furnishings and curtains and echoes in accessories like pillows, curtain tape, and rug—then crowns it all off with *Kubilai's Tent wallpaper by Iksel Decorative Arts through Schumacher* on the ceiling.

In a sitting area of the same Southampton house shown on the preceding page, Manger reprises *Kubilai's Tent by Iksel Decorative Arts (available through Schumacher)* on the walls and quietly echoes its linearity throughout the room—in striped upholstery, the frames of rattan armchairs, a chevron-stripe rug, and shiplap paneling on the ceiling—to make it all feel of a piece.

CHARMING

NEVER UNDERESTIMATE THE POWER OF A ROOM THAT MAKES YOU SMILE.
VERY FEW APPROACHES CREATE SUCH INSTANT EASE—AND AT THE END
OF A LONG DAY, ISN'T EASE PRECISELY THE POINT? IT JUST SO HAPPENS
THAT BLUE AND WHITE ARE TONAL TOOLS THAT PULL IN THE CHARM LIKE
NOBODY'S BUSINESS. ACROSS THEIR BROAD RANGE, IN NEARLY EVERY
SHADE AND DEPTH, THEY'RE FRIENDLY, FELICITOUS COLORS, TAILOR-MADE
FOR FORGING ROOMS THAT MAKE YOU HAPPY. WHAT COULD BE BETTER?

In Charles and Olya Thompson's Brooklyn home, wooden floorboards cloaked in white, judicious pops of red, and an intriguing portrait make a bedroom enveloped in punchy damask a sweetly sophisticated escape. PRECEDING PAGES: Miranda Brooks's and architect Bastien Halard's daughters look impishly at home in their Brooklyn abode, where a cerulean bedstead echoes the foliage wallpaper (Chestnut by Marthe Armitage) that's a just-so shade of grayish teal blue.

Mining a Provençal vein in the Pacific Palisades, Mark D. Sikes, combines earthy materials like terra-cotta and deeply burnished woods with artfully painted plates and fabrics—including *Schumacher's Cabanon Stripe*—in a simple, evocative vignette that's more than the sum of its parts. OPPOSITE: A collection of cream-colored porcelain and ceramics is brought to life with *Marella wallpaper by Vogue Living for Schumacher*.

In this serene and sybaritic scheme at the ASH NYC-designed Peter and Paul Hotel in New Orleans—composed almost entirely of ginghams in varying scales—checks really *do* mark the spot.

With scalloped shades and a bow, an almost-too-pretty painted tole sconce might threaten toothache; Angelica Squire masterfully pulls it in the opposite direction with fun-loving but gutsy *Spotted Star wallpaper by Molly Mahon for Schumacher*. OPPOSITE: *Schumacher's Floweret wallcovering* in a chalky gray hue and a statement-making sink in dusty blue give this Charlotte powder room by Georgia Street an artful sense of depth.

A pared-down guest room in the home of Pat Guthman designed
by John Scoville is wrapped entirely in shades of ivory—save
for the interior of the bed canopies and accompanying skirts, like
a surprise boon reserved for lucky weekend visitors. OPPOSITE:
With its sheath of white plaster, a cheery check (*Agnes
Sheer by Vogue Living for Schumacher*) is practically the only
embellishment needed in this rustic upstate New York bathroom.

A warm and weathered wooden farm table elevated by porcelain and slipcovers and napkins (in *Marella* and *Bunny fabrics by Vogue Living for Schumacher*) proves that even measured doses can make a powerfully pretty impact. OPPOSITE: This kitchen by Studio Dorion composed of traditional elements—shiplap paneling, spatter-painted floors, pleated cabinet curtains—strikes a subtly minimalist tone, distilling function to its barest form before leavening it with pure enchanting color.

SPARE &
SENSUAL

THE LESS-IS-MORE CAMP OF DECORATING CAN BE DECEPTIVELY COMPLEX:
YOUR FLOOR PLANS ARE SO SEEMINGLY SIMPLE, YOUR SCHEMES SO ELEMENTAL
THAT ANYONE FROM THE MAXIMALIST SCHOOL OF THOUGHT MIGHT BELIEVE
THAT FURNISHING WITH A MINIMUM OF MATERIALS IS A PIECE OF CAKE. BUT
ANYONE WHO'S A PROPONENT OF EDITING KNOWS THAT THE MORE YOU TAKE
OUT OF A ROOM, THE MORE IMPACTFUL ANYTHING LEFT BEHIND BECOMES,
WHICH MEANS THOSE PIECES HAVE TO BRING THEIR A GAME TO THE FESTIVITIES
OR THE DESIGN WILL FALL FLAT. IT'S ALSO WHY BLUE AND WHITE SHOULD
BECOME A MAJOR TOOL IN YOUR PARED-DOWN ARSENAL: THE COMBINATION WILL
GIVE YOU THE DEPTH AND DIMENSION YOU CRAVE WITHOUT A WHIFF OF FUSS.

Whether it's a refined antique bust, an angular
canopy bed, a shapely center table, or a twisting
architectural model of a staircase, each item in this
Bruce Budd–designed room has such a strong sculp-
tural presence that little else is needed. PRECEDING
PAGE: Jason Arnold achieves a similar subtlety in a
show house bedroom that speaks volumes with a
minimum of flourishes. The pediment-shaped bed is
upholstered in *Schumacher's Morrison ticking stripe*.

In his former carriage house, Bruce Budd created an artful composition with wide plank floors, blue-chip French antiques, and an exacting scheme that relies almost entirely on blue and white to achieve its serene elegance.

In a Jacksonville, Florida, space defined by quality—the door
and its hardware, the gilt console, the lantern—Stephanie
Jarvis saves room for a single embellishment with *Sepiessa
by Caroline Z. Hurley for Schumacher* on the settee, which
makes the whole thing sing. OPPOSITE: Stephen Sills's noble
interpretation of classical architecture in Bedford, New York,
achieves a quiet kind of splendor with chalky walls in weathered
Prussian blue and a monolithic door surround and pediment.

A curved sofa in marine-blue velvet and an op-art rug lend a sense
of swirling movement to the living room of an 18th-century apartment
in Paris's Eighth Arrondissement, designed by Studio KO. OPPOSITE:
Jacques Grange punctuates classical architecture with a sublimely
sinuous staircase and modern art; a pair of Louis XVI chairs
is the delicate robin's-egg-blue icing on the nearly all-white cake.

TRADITIONAL

IN CERTAIN CIRCLES, THE WORD *TRADITIONAL* HAS BECOME SYNONYMOUS
WITH FUSTY AND OLD. NOTHING COULD BE FURTHER FROM THE TRUTH: WE'RE
GUESSING THAT THOSE NAYSAYERS HAVE NEVER CONSIDERED THE SURPRISINGLY
SLEEK LINES OF A GEORGE III SIDEBOARD OR ENCOUNTERED THE UNADULTERATED
SPLENDOR OF A REGENCY MIRROR. AND THEY'VE CERTAINLY NEVER WITNESSED
THE WONDER THAT BLUE AND WHITE CAN RENDER FOR ROOMS THAT LOOK
MORE TO THE PAST THAN THEY DO TO INSTAGRAM FOR INSPIRATION, AWASH IN
AN AIRY LIGHTNESS THAT BRIGHTENS WHATEVER IT TOUCHES. IN OTHER WORDS,
THE VERY OPPOSITE OF FUSTY. EAT YOUR HEART OUT, MR. AND MRS. EAMES.

Crawford Linen check by Williamsburg for Schumacher is the perfect complement
to the blue-and-white Delftware fireplace surround in the 18th-century Wynkoop
House in Pound Ridge, New York. OPPOSITE: Using a busy pattern under the eaves
is a tried-and-true decorator's trick to make a space feel cozy and pulled together.
Here, *Schumacher's Indian Arbre fabric* was paper-backed and hung like wallpaper
on both the ceiling and walls. PRECEDING PAGES: Enamored of *Schumacher's
Hydrangea Drape wallpaper* since spotting it in *Gone with the Wind*, Amy Studebaker
made it the focal point of a powder room in her St. Louis house, matching
its hues for the vanity and mirror and using brass hardware for a dash of contrast.

Blue and white pairs particularly well with dark wood
antiques, as evidenced by Tom Helme's bathroom and
dressing room at his home in England, where he upholstered
the walls in a handsome stripe. Bright red trim hides the
seams, emphasizes the architecture, and adds a note of
surprise. OPPOSITE: In Frank DiBiasi's New York bedroom,
a mahogany chair mingles beautifully with a striped wall
and a door painted in two complementary shades of blue.

Jenny Holladay of Summer Thornton Design gives elegant gilt antiques a healthy dose of fresh spring air with *Schumacher's famed Pyne Hollyhock* on the walls of her Chicago living room, layering in more pattern with pleated lampshades and a ruffled armchair (*Schumacher's Salisbury Chintz*) for a stylish effect that seems generations in the making.

In New York, Miles Redd goes all out with Gustavian gusto, showcasing a selection of Swedish antiques with a fitting, flowery backdrop that goes particularly well with their distinctive painted chalky finishes.

A bed canopy in a blowsy Bennison linen and contemporary art above the mantel supplies this London bedroom by Veere Grenney a bracing sensibility that has no time stamp. OPPOSITE: In the drawing room of his Georgetown town house, Frank Babb Randolph deployed shades of blue, white, and greige as a neutral backdrop to make French and English antiques feel positively modern.

Mary McDonald's fanciful *Chinois Palais wallpaper for Schumacher* takes
pride of place in a Greenwich, Connecticut, dining room by Samantha Varvel,
giving an antique sideboard, mirror, and chairs (in *Schumacher's Elton check*)
an enchanting new lease on life. OPPOSITE: Jill Lasersohn's butler's pantry
is old-fashioned in the best sense of the word, its clean lines enlivened
by a ruffled cabinet curtain in her *Toile de la Prairie fabric for Schumacher*.

For her daughter's bedroom in Dallas, Amy Berry
softened the gleam of a gilt Louis XVI–style bed with
Schumacher's Versailles wallpaper, for a quiet, calm,
and comforting aura. OPPOSITE: With Schumacher's
neoclassical-leaning *Fern Tree wallpaper*, Lizzie Cullen Cox
graciously updates a vintage-style ball-and-foot bathtub.

EXUBERANT

SOMETIMES, A ROOM JUST WANTS TO MAKE AN ENTRANCE, TURN HEADS, OR CALL
ATTENTION TO ITSELF. WE GET IT—DECORATING SHOULDN'T JUST BE A BACKDROP.
IF YOU'RE FROM THE SHOUT-IT-FROM-THE-ROOFTOPS SCHOOL OF INTERIORS,
THEN YOU KNOW THAT THE SECRET TO SUCCESS IS KNOWING WHEN TO SAY WHEN.
AND NOTHING WILL TAME A SPLASHY PRINT OR STATEMENT-MAKING PIECE LIKE
SENSIBLY SENSUAL BLUE AND WHITE. LIKE THAT VOICE INSIDE YOUR HEAD THAT TELLS
YOU TO TAKE ONE THING OFF BEFORE WALKING OUT THE DOOR, A CONTROLLED
PALETTE CAN BE THE DIFFERENCE BETWEEN EFFERVESCENCE AND EXCESS.

To conquer the odd proportions of a pitched ceiling in an East Hampton, New York, bedroom, Lucy Doswell went all out with a leafy Meg Braff wallpaper that might have been overwhelming were it not for its soothing seaglass shade. OPPOSITE: A fancy crenellated canopy tops a metal four-poster bed in a Sea Island, Georgia, bedroom by James Michael Howard; he gives it just the lightest punch with cerulean edging and a similarly intense hue on the upholstered bench. PRECEDING PAGES: The Vase, Clarence House's oversize David Hicks–designed print, takes center stage in this Watch Hill, Rhode Island, hallway by Tom Scheerer, dramatically framing a Jud Hartmann bust of Sassacus, the last chief of the Pequot tribe.

Schumacher's Leaf Stripe wallpaper makes quite a statement in this dormered guest room by Suzanne Lovell, and thanks to blue and white, it's surprisingly soothing, too. OPPOSITE: Paired with an oversize fretwork runner and lively abstract art, Patrick and Meghan Sharp make *Schumacher's Iconic Leopard wallpaper* roar winningly in Serenbe, Georgia.

A Salt Lake City bedroom by the Fox Group is a childhood daydream come true, whisking its inhabitant away to an enchanted garden through a combination of floral fabric-covered walls (*Schumacher's Garden Gate chintz*), creamy treillage, and plenty of picnic-perfect gingham (*Schumacher's Bermuda Check*) that keeps everything in, well, check.

Classic fretwork (*Schumacher's Octavia Paperweave wallcovering*) and florals (*Schumacher's Bouquet Chinois fabric*) harmonize effortlessly in a Chicago home office by Shelley Johnstone. OPPOSITE: In her New York bedroom, Lilly Bunn goes for playful pattern-on-pattern (with *Schumacher's Fern Tree wallpaper* and *Bouquet Chinois fabric*) without going over the top.

ICONIC DESIGNS

WHETHER YOUR TASTE LEANS MORE BOLD OR BREEZY, THERE'S NO SHORTAGE
OF WAYS TO BRING CLASSIC BLUE-AND-WHITE STYLE INTO YOUR OWN ABODE.
NOT SURE WHERE TO BEGIN? IN THE FOLLOWING PAGES, YOU'LL FIND A BEVY OF
OPTIONS—IN THE FORM OF CHINA AND PORCELAIN, WALLPAPERS AND FABRICS—
THAT ARE TRIED-AND-TESTED (SOME ACROSS CENTURIES), ENTHRALLINGLY
INVENTIVE, OR SIMPLY QUINTESSENTIAL. FROM ARTFUL SPLATTERS AND GRAPHIC
STRIPES TO CHEERY CHINOISERIES AND OLD-FASHIONED BLOOMS, THESE TIMELESS
MOTIFS WILL SATISFY EVERY POSSIBLE YEN. ALLEZ LES BLEUS (AND BLANCS)!

OISEAU BLEU
Gien

BLUE CANTON
Mottahedeh

BLUE ITALIAN
Spode

BLUE ONION
Meissen

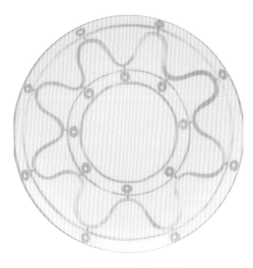

SERENITY BLUE
Themis Z

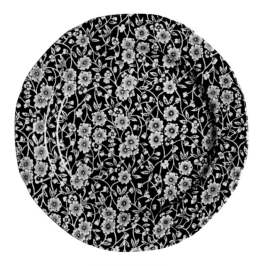

BLUE CALICO
Burleigh

ICONIC TABLEWARE

BLUE FLUTED FULL LACE
Royal Copenhagen

ARABESQUE
Dansk

WILLOW BLUE
Johnson Brothers

GALERIE ROYALE BLEU NUIT
Bernardaud

CHINESE BOUQUET BLUE
Herend

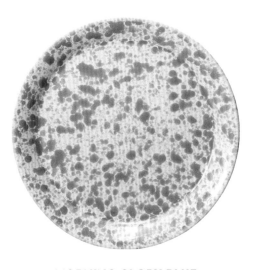

MORNING GLORY BLUE
Bennington Potters

TALAVERA
Brunschwig & Fils

THE VASE
Clarence House

FEATHER BLOOM SISAL
Celerie Kemble for Schumacher

SERENDIPITY
Sister Parish

DESMOND
Sister Parish

KATSUGI
Schumacher

ICONIC WALLPAPERS

HYDRANGEA DRAPE
Schumacher

TIBET
Clarence House

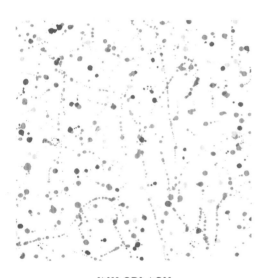

INK SPLASH
Porter Teleo for Schumacher

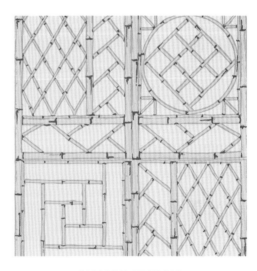

LYFORD TRELLIS
China Seas for Quadrille

DOLLY
Sister Parish

FERN TREE
Schumacher

PYNE HOLLYHOCK
Schumacher

BIRD & THISTLE
Brunschwig & Fils

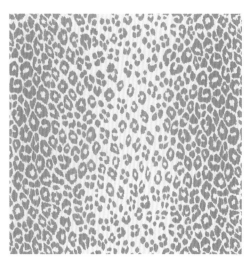

ICONIC LEOPARD
Schumacher

CHENONCEAU
Schumacher

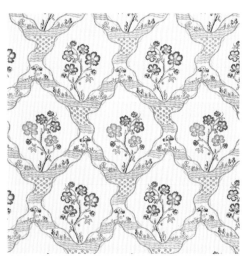

MARELLA
Vogue Living for Schumacher

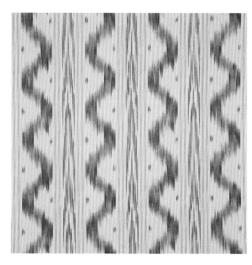

TOILE DE NANTES
Pierre Frey

ICONIC **FABRICS**

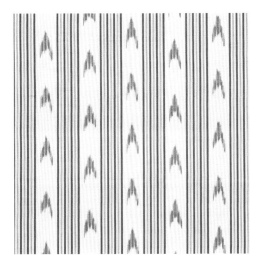

SANTA BARBARA IKAT
Mark D. Sikes for Schumacher

CHIANG MAI DRAGON
Schumacher

EXOTIC BUTTERFLY
Schumacher

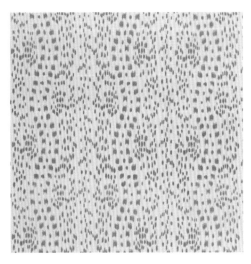

LES TOUCHES
Brunschwig & Fils

SAMARKAND IKAT II
Schumacher

ARBRE DE MATISSE
China Seas for Quadrille

ACKNOWLEDGMENTS

I WOULD LIKE TO EXTEND MY GRATITUDE TO THE FOLLOWING INDIVIDUALS WHO HELPED MAKE THIS BOOK POSSIBLE:

DARA CAPONIGRO FOR YOUR LEADERSHIP, INSPIRATION, AND SUPPORT. THANK YOU FOR TAKING A CHANCE ON ME RIGHT OUT OF COLLEGE AND FOR GUIDING ME THROUGH THIS PROCESS WITH YOUR BOUNTY OF EXPERIENCE.

EMMA BAZILIAN AND STEPHANIE DIAZ FOR BEING MY PARTNERS IN CRIME. THANK YOU FOR YOUR GUIDANCE AND SKILL AND WIT AND GENIUS.

MARIO LÓPEZ-CORDERO FOR THE BEAUTIFUL WORDS THAT HELPED BRING THESE IMAGES TO LIFE.

ELLA CHARKES FOR YOUR TIRELESS EFFORTS TO PROCURE THE PHOTOGRAPHS FEATURED IN THESE PAGES.

TIMUR YUMUSAKLAR FOR ALLOWING ME TO EXPLORE AND CREATE UNDER THE INCREDIBLE UMBRELLA OF FS&CO.

JESSICA TOLMACH FOR LEADING US INTO THE WORLD OF BOOK PUBLISHING.

THE SCHUMACHER DESIGN STUDIO FOR CREATING SO MANY BEAUTIFUL TEXTILES AND WALLPAPERS.

THE INCREDIBLE DESIGNERS WHOSE INTERIORS INSPIRE ME EVERY DAY.

THE TALENTED PHOTOGRAPHERS WHO SO MASTERFULLY CAPTURED EACH OF THESE SPACES.

THE SCHUMACHER, POZIER, AND PUSCHEL FAMILIES FOR BUILDING AND STEWARDING THIS COMPANY FOR MORE THAN 134 YEARS.

THE SCHUMACHER BOARD OF DIRECTORS FOR YOUR DEDICATION TO SCHUMACHER AND CARRYING IT INTO THE 21ST CENTURY AND BEYOND.

AND, FINALLY, TO MY FRIENDS AND FAMILY FOR YOUR SUPPORT AND LOVE. I COULDN'T DO ANY OF THIS WITHOUT YOU.

PHOTOGRAPHY

William Abranowicz (P. 98) Melanie Acevedo (PP. 18, 51, 54–55, 77, 84, 121, 122) Brittany Ambridge/OTTO (P. 114) Gieves Anderson/Trunk Archive (P. 62–63) J. Ashley Photography (P. 117) Dylan Chandler (P. 42) Paloma Contreras (P. 57) Paul Costello (P. 0) Kip Dawkins (P. 111) Peter Dolkas (P. 85) Michael Dunne, 1993/Oak Spring Garden Foundation, Upperville, VA (PP. 60–61) Holger Ellgaard (P. 7) Richard Felber (PP. 88–89, 90–91) Emily Followill (P. 86) Josh Gibson (P. 25) François Halard (P. 99) François Halard/Creative Exchange Agency (PP. 72, 74–75, 94, 95) Christian Harder (PP. 78–79) Stephen Kent Johnson/OTTO (P. 64) Stephan Julliard (PP. 37, 38, 44) Stephen Karlisch (P. 48) Erin Kestenbaum (P. 109) Max Kim-Bee (PP. 4, 24, 41, 52–53) Max Kim-Bee/OTTO (PP. 30–31, 67, 106) Francesco Lagnese (PP. 40, 102–103, 108, 120) Francesco Lagnese/OTTO (PP. 43, 68–69, 70–71, 112, 115) Sean Litchfield (P. 32) Thomas Loof/Art Department (PP. 20, 58–59) Yana Marudova (P. 11) Michael Mundy (PP. 26–27) Heather Nan (P. 56) Amy Neunsinger (PP. 16, 19, 76) Alise O'Brien (P. 96) Courtney Parker (P. 33) David Phelps, House Beautiful, Hearst Magazine Media, Inc. (P. 83) Eric Piasecki/OTTO (P. 116) Greg Premru (P. 45) Jessie Preza (P. 92) Will Reid Interiors (P. 23) Celia Rogge (P. 9) Lindsay Salazar (PP. 118, 119) Nick Sargent (P. 49) Annie Schlechter (P. 21) Annie Schlechter, Courtesy of The Colonial Williamsburg Foundation (P. 2) Nathan Schroder (P. 110) Ingalill Snitt (P. 8) Angelica Squire (P. 81) Laura Sumrak (P. 80) Christopher Simon Sykes/The Interior Archive x Trunk Archive (P. 101) Simon Upton/The Interior Archive x Trunk Archive (PP. 66, 104–105) Simon Upton/Trunk Archive (PP. 100, 107) William Waldron (P. 82) William Waldron/OTTO (PP. 29, 34–35, 93) Bjorn Wallander/OTTO (PP. 22, 28, 46, 50) Elsa Young (P. 36)

OPENING PAGES

OPENING IMAGE: In his Los Angeles kitchen, Johnson Hartig of fashion label Libertine mounts actual Delftware on his trompe l'oeil *Plates and Platters wallpaper for Schumacher*, for what you might call a tongue-in-chic effect. PAGE 2: Swathed in *Lafayette Botanical fabric by Williamsburg for Schumacher*, a Heather Chadduck–designed bedroom at the Nelson-Galt House in Colonial Williamsburg feels utterly cocooning—and remarkably calming. PAGE 4: Schumacher's flowing pictorial *Pearl River wallpaper* imbues a bedroom with happy whimsy, while a diffuse stripe on the headboard (*Moncorvo linen by David Oliver for Schumacher*) and a galvanized stool used as an end table keep the scheme from going over the top.

COVER

Exotic Butterfly fabric by Schumacher

ENDPAPERS

Astral wallpaper by Schumacher

First published in the United States in 2023 by Schumacher Books
Frederic Media
459 Broadway
New York, NY 10013

Distributed by Monacelli
A Phaidon Company
111 Broadway
New York, NY 10006

Blue and White Done Right: The Classic Color Combination for Every Decorating Style
Copyright © 2023 Schumacher Books
Photography copyright © artists
Produced by Hudson Moore
Art directed by Stephanie Diaz
Written by Mario López-Cordero
Edited by Emma Bazilian
Publisher: Frederic Media
Editorial Director: Dara Caponigro

Printed in China
ISBN: 978-1-58093-635-4
Library of Congress Control Number: 2023936959

Visit us online:
schumacher.com
instagram.com/schumacher1889
youtube.com/schumacher1889
pinterest.com/schumacher1889